USELYSSES

Chapbooks by Noel Black

Night Falls/Under Days
This Is the Strange Part
Solar Donuts (with Will Yackulic & Ed Berrigan)
Vacancy
Shoplifter's Honor
Hulktrans
In the City of Word People

Noel Black

Uselysses

Ugly Duckling Presse • Brooklyn, New York

In the City of Word People was originally published as a chapbook by Blue Press in 2008. "8 Dead Poets" was originally published as a pamphlet by Furniture Press. "Poem" and "Another Poem" were published in *Try* in 2009. "Aubade," "Poem on my 36th Birthday," "When God Created Pigeons," and "If I Had a Super Power" were originally published in *Nevada State Line* in 2009. "Insect Dust," "Poem of Carl Sagan," "They Say You Need a Slogan for Christmas," "When Physicists Finally Discover Irreducible Matter," and "Behind This Groucho Marx Disguise" were first published in *Big Bell* in 2010.

Library of Congress Cataloging-in-Publication Data

Black, Noel, 1972-
  Uselysses / Noel Black. – 1st ed.
    p. cm.
  ISBN 978-1-933254-89-0 (pbk. : alk. paper)
  I. Title.
  PS3602.L32523U84 2011
  811'.6–dc23
                              2011029356

First Edition, First Printing.

Printed in the United States of America
at McNaughton & Gunn in Saline, MI.

Cover images by Streeter Wright, lettering by Marina Eckler.
Design by SoA.

Ugly Duckling Presse
232 Third Street, #E002
Brooklyn, NY 11215
uglyducklingpresse.org

Distributed to the trade by
Small Press Distribution
spdbooks.org

This book was partially funded by a grant
from the New York State Council on the Arts.
State of the Arts

NYSCA

for Marina

CONTENTS

When Physicists Finally Discover Irreducible Matter
Grape Iris
I Used to Get Lost in the Saying
Thou Art My Dearest Deer
Insect Dust
Once Upon a Time
Ouroboros
Vija Celmins & The Case of the Nocturnal Pocketbook
Poem
Nothing Always Happens
Championship Champagne Bologna
Poem of Carl Sagan
Praise for Penis Jonson
Sausage Ice
Uselysses

Moby K. Dick
Lord Jim Thompson
Paul Austerlitz
Watchmen in the Rye
Huckleberry Finnegans Wake
The Spy Who Came in from the Cold Blood
The Thief's Journals of Lewis & Clark
Notes from Under the Volcano
Remembrance of the Amnesiac
Slaughterhouse 2666
Pinocchiorwell
Farenheit 49
Miss Lonelyhearts of Darkness
Fredrick X-Men
Pierre Menard, Author of The Capote
George Sandman
A Cloud Atlas Is Hard to Find
Journey to the End of Ulysses

(Because you are greasy or pimpled, or were once drunk, or a thief,
Or that you are diseas'd, or rheumatic, or a prostitute,
Or from frivolity or impotence, or that you are no scholar and never
    saw your name in print,
Do you give in that you are any less immortal?)

—Walt Whitman, "A Song for Occupations"

IN THE CITY OF WORD PEOPLE

In the Manner of Gerard Manley Hopkins, Sort Of

Even the most mundane
of what already exists
without artifice
seems more interesting to me
than anything we might
strive to create.
These lines, for instance,
don't hold the light like the lilac
bush—long out of bloom here
in late summer, just a riot
of shaggy green, overgrown,
dappled like some Hopkins consonance
I can't even approach.
I wish I had time to work
on my zombie novel
down at Dunkin' Donuts
all day long.

Poem for Marina

I was saying something about a painting of a figure skater on an ice floe

& you said you once wrote a poem about a car crash on an ice floe.

Now I'm writing this poem about it while you paint a picture of an
archipelago of Pysanky eggs and tatted honeycomb hills adrift in an
incomplete arctic sea.

I like looking at your egg cartons of gouache because I don't understand
color:

salmony pink next to brown next to Hulk green next to cadmium orange
not like words at all, well … I don't even know what that means.

"Oh, melancholy!" Ursen said yesterday as we shuffled through the field
at Whitney's grandmother's in Calhan where the black grasshoppers
with the cadmium orange wings rose from the Hulk green alfalfa as the
sand burrs stuck to his socks.

He also called The Beach Boys "The Beach Brothers" and lost a tooth
and learned to ride his bike without training wheels.

I feel upset with this poem for everything it cannot be, which is
everything around me right now: you and all our memories.

Disillusionment

The daffodils don't look as yellow
as they used to, nor does the AT&T/Sprint
awning across the street look as orange
as it did just a few minutes ago
before the sugar crash from the Dr. Pepper
I drank at lunch. Chainsaw Hitler has a blue plastic lei
around his neck and a fake Pancho Villa moustache
over his Hitler moustache. Some people even think
he's Pancho Villa on vacation in Hawaii. Fools!
The grains of wood on his face are like
the waves of the Pacific Ocean
passing gently over the white sand beaches at Lani Kai
where my son found a long, rubbery piece of kelp
he used to whip pigeons during John Dicker's wedding
a couple years ago. It was a really beautiful wedding.
They're still married and plan on having children soon.
Children who probably won't use long pieces of rubbery kelp
to whip pigeons on the white sandy beaches of Lani Kai.

8 Dead Poets

Walt Whitman

Whitman's lines traversed the page like settlers on the plains
Marking an immeasurable space in his Manifest Destiny brain

But when the Good Gray Poet died they took his big brain out
& tried to measure, but dropped it—oops! & splattered it all about

Vladimir Mayakovsky

The odds: 1 to 6
Against River Styx

His brains got sprayed
& Death got paid.

Sylvia Plath

Turned on the gath.

Percy Bysshe Shelley

The death of Keats the year before
Then Mary lost one baby more
With Hope, more so than death, a bore
His body washed up on the shore

Obscure it came—his drowning fate—
The Hope that poets legislate

Emily Dickinson

Death kindly stopped
& on She—hopped

Arthur Rimbaud

He died 2 deaths, Arthur Rimbaud
The first when just 19:
　　His perfidious breath
　　Crossed the River of Lethe
(On a drunken boat was last seen)

18 years more, his body died,
Though he longed to sail back to Harrar
"In a boat as frail as a May butterfly" …
"Let it be the Aphinar"

Alexander Pushkin

The blood of Russians and African slaves
Spilled in Pushkin's early grave

Typical romantic fool—
Took a slug in the gut at a petty love duel

Just like Lenski in *Onegin* did—
His book a prophetic coffin lid.

Frank O'Hara

"If I had my way I'd go on & on
and never go to sleep,"
said Frank O'Hara just hours before
he got hit by a Jeep.

Something Ron Padgett Said to Me in an Interview

Is that a poem can be anything, which is why, he said
people still write poetry. I tend to agree with him,
though it's certainly disappointing that poems can't
make people stop being assholes, or end greed and suffering or
alleviate that uncomfortable chafing I get in my perineum
after a long summertime bicycle ride through the rolling
hills of Garden of the Gods here in Colorado Springs
where the hog backs rise up from the ground
like the spines of petrified dragons
who slumber just below the crust of the earth. Actually,
the spires of sandy red rock here are petrified river beds
pushed up on end by a geological process called
"folding," which I don't fully understand, though I
like to think about the ancient rivers that ran across them.
And I like to imagine those same rivers
running swiftly across them now, vertically!
With that shimmering glint that comes off the tips of rivulets
in a blathering creek in some canyon or another somewhere
as I ride past it on my silver bicycle
like an ancient river running vertically and swiftly away
from assholes and greed and suffering and poetry.

There's a Wren Perched on the Back of My Toilet

There's a wren perched on the back of my toilet
thinking about going for a jaunty little boat ride
on a little wooden balloon boat with a red flag
through the fjords in Norway where quaint villages
cling to the lush green hills, far from Colorado Springs
where the climate is arid, but not unpleasant,
though there's nothing really quaint at all about this city.
This city makes me very angry, actually, as I live in it
like a little sugar person inside a sugar egg
that my mother gave me for Easter, which I promptly
threw in the trash because I hate sugar eggs. Well, hate
is maybe too strong a word when the wren is not
a real wren, but a wooden wren.

                                       He is fake, but affable
upon his little log and next to the wooden balloon boat
just beneath the picture of the fjords, a very relaxing picture
my wife found at the thrift store, which hangs above the toilet.
This is what's real! The picture of the cruise ship on which real people
were probably having sex at the moment the photographer snapped
that photo from the lush green hills high above. Who cares
about the scenery—if only we had a telescope, we could see them
doing it like tiny rabbits inside a sugar egg. You can't
escape your life for long, I think, as I stare at the objects
that became the scenery and characters
in this play of my brief fantasy
as I sit in the bathtub like a cruise ship in a fjord
that promises to carry me far far away

from whatever it is I can't seem to figure out.

The Meaning of Life Is Dolphins

The camp years were over when Rock Hudson came out
to promote Doris Day's new television program
looking like a Holocaust apology, thought Bert Swanson
to himself as he pulled up to the stoplight
at the corner of 21ST Street and Hwy 24.

"The meaning of life is to live it!" said a bumper sticker
on the red Dodge Stratus in front of him.
He also noticed a clear blue crystal dolphin
dangling from the rear view mirror.

"The meaning of life is dolphins,"
he muttered under his breath as the light changed
and he stepped on the gas with purpose,
driving recklessly past the new fly-fishing shop
that had just opened up
at the corner of 21ST Street and Hwy 24
on his way home home to pick up his racquetball bag.

A Young Poet Recently Approached Me

A young poet recently approached me in a bar
to say he liked my poems,
which is something that every poet
looks forward to when he is still
a young poet.

It was flattering. He had read a couple of my poems
in some student literary journal.
Bright-eyed and newly bearded, a completely
affable fellow, he used to be in a
brilliant tech-violence mathcore band
called The Great Redneck Hope.

I interviewed them once and they
showed me pictures from their tour called
"Poopin' 'n' Stuff" during which they had
top-shelved toilets across the country,
which means taking a shit in the septic tank
rather than in the toilet bowl proper.
Cheeky!

His lyrics never struck me as anything special,
but it hardly mattered since they weren't discernible
through the brilliant squawking.
His spastic kinesis on stage was fantastic.
He really had something—
"charisma" is too lazy a word.
Girls would present themselves naked in the tour van
in hopes of being touched, however briefly,
by his centaurian need.

The band was a total bore after they kicked him out.
His only talents were beauty and abandon.

More than enough! I thought, but it was time
to hunker down and get serious about poetry.

You're Just a Stupid Specialist

I love to read the poems of James Schuyler
even though I envy the seeming bourgeois repose
he seems to have enjoyed while writing them. Of course,
he was schizophrenic, and I can't even pretend
to imagine where that's concerned. But someone—
I think it might have been Joanne Kyger—
once said of his writing: "The details made up
for the damage," which made sense.

I have a copy of *The Morning of the Poem*,
paperback, third edition on Farrar, Straus and Giroux.
The cover is sort of boring and wonderful—a black and white
drawing of an amaryllis set in a window
against a modern apartment building,
which is very Schuyler. Lines like:

"   … The fields
beyond the feeding sparrows are
brown, palely brown yet with an inward glow
like that of someone of a frank good nature
whom you trust. I want to hear the music
hanging in the air and drink my
Coca-Cola."

The binding has long-since dried up
and little crumbs of the yellow glue
fall into my chest hairs as I read it in bed
next to my wife and son, who said to me earlier:

"You're just a stupid specialist who went to high school."

Sometimes I Do Feel Genuinely Happy

Looking out my office window right now,
there is a lovely Russian sage bush
with purple flowers underneath a stately maple tree
covered in Virginia creeper. I see all of this through
the slats in the venetian blinds, and it pleases me for reasons
I can't quite figure—maybe it's the idea of something
beautiful inside a frame excluding the horror
of everything else, though that would be overstating it
somewhat.

Looking down from this view at my computer
where I have teenpinkvideos.com open in my browser, I see
it's a boring lesbian scene starring
Eva and Jennifer who are giving it to one another
with red and blue jelly rubber dildos respectively.
Eva has pretty nice tits and I like her braids, but
Jennifer's slightly discolored egg-shaped nipples
bug me. The white, faux Roman banister that rises from right
to left across the screen behind them along with the ferns on either
side of the couch make for a decent composition, but that hideous
jungle pattern upholstery doesn't do much for their pussies.

One thing I hate about poetry is the stately voice
you imagine while writing, as though you're
standing at a lectern in a distinguished auditorium
on a university campus in a quaint mid-western town
in front of hundreds of intelligent and thoughtful people
who actually give a shit.

An E-mail to Nico Alvarado-Greenwood

Even if it is sort of Billy Collinsy,
I like a conversational tone in my poems lately,
and I like them to be about my very few thoughts
about poetry, or to have a sort of
hissing whispered aside quality
that you might hear
under the breath of some grumpy jerk
at a terrible poetry reading.

I hardly ever write poems
anymore, and there has always been
this feeling that I couldn't figure out
what was wrong with them
when they didn't work.

I try to be honest to my thoughts, but line breaks
can feel so arbitrary, or …
something else I don't get.
For example, I could almost line-out
this paragraph into a poem:

Anyhow in the "Genuinely Happy" poem,
I was noticing the lyrical scenery
in two completely different contexts
kind of like seeing a Fairfield Porter
and an Eric Fischl painting at the same museum
because it was true, not because
I want it to be jarring,
though I'm certainly often jarred
by comprehending the gestalt inherent
in the layers of my own perceiving.

You don't have to workshop my poems
when I send them to you, y'know?

We used to just give them to each other
and publish them and see what happened,
which usually wasn't much. "I like this, I
don't like that, etc." But there
was a conversation about style and what
worked and what didn't in the books and magazines.
The workshops always got too far
from the impulse for me. I always thought
poetry was more about friendship. But poetry can be
anything, as Ron Padgett once told me, i.e.
there are no real rules other than what works,
which this doesn't, though, I would guess,
it's why people still write poetry.

Like Aaron Menza laying out his rug on dirt.

And then I could title it something like "A Poem for
    Nico Alvarado-Greenwood"

And then you would publish it in a magazine called "Green Wood"

And then we would go have a beer

and talk about something else.

In the City of Word People

William Blake's dick is where the money is.
The country of hand to mouth songs
losing the picture I cannot get
under a log for the dead.
A pale wrinkle in bad decline—
horrible beautiful night of the living Hitlers.

Under the world, Satan's riverboat of indecision collects the air,
killing without glory or punishment.

Who can collect the wolf?

Brighty, nighty, disappointment writing
in the heart you can't win.

This is the poem I wrote while sort of half-staring
at the bookshelf beside my bed.
I used to like to think about books being neighbors
on bookshelves, which were like skyscrapers of books,
and that inside your house was a metropolis of word people
even if you lived in a log cabin by yourself
in the middle of a beautiful meadow
so beautiful that every time you looked out your window
you would think about the Robert Duncan poem
"Often I Am Permitted to Return to a Meadow"
even though you were already in a meadow
surrounded by thousands of wonderful books
written by people you're glad don't live there.

THE INNER CITY

If I Had a Super Power

If I had a super power
it would be a moustache so amazing
it could sweep away crime
like a mighty broom
emanating from my upper lip.

It would also dispatch with jerks & chores &
bad feelings—like the one I'm having right now
that has me in a headlock
as it delivers a painful noogie and cackles maniacally:
"You shoudn't have moved to New York City, dumbass!"

I remember driving across Iowa in our Budget moving van
& wondering if anyone else speeding eastward on I-80
thought of the highway as Walt Whitman's dead gray tongue
laid out across the landscape
as we barreled backwards
against its manifested destiny.

"Maybe these jerks at the Iowa Writer's Workshop,"
I thought as we stopped in Iowa City
for a bowl of noodles and a comic book
about a superhero who murders the president
out of genuine patriotism in order to restore democracy and free elections.

"I would definitely murder the president with my moustache broom!"
I think as I sit at my desk in New York City,
if I could just get out of this headlock.

Children of Children of Adam
—for Alysia Abbott

I've been meaning to reread Whitman since we moved to Brooklyn a
    month ago,

so I finally pull down this strange beige Heritage Editions Reprints
    complete and unabridged hardcover edition *ex libris* Dorothy Anne
    Naskin with illustrations by Rockwell Kent that my grandmother gave
    me years ago.

It doesn't have a publication date & only a strange preface from George
    Macy, Director of The Heritage Club, explaining that the smaller
    margins and thinner paper have been used so as to comply with the
    government's wartime regulation governing reprints.

Also, there's this strange image on the title page that cleverly spells
    "WW" in grass sprouting out of a black block that contains the
    cryptic numbers 8611776 and 6071492 respectively in a deco font,
    which I imagine for a moment are the clues to George Washington
    and Christopher Columbus' posthumous Masonic cell phone
    numbers in a teen time travel super-hero history mystery ...

Anyway, I don't love this edition, but it's the only one I've got, and it's
    getting late,

so I flip open to "Children of Adam" on page 96 and read:

"The boy's longings, the glow and pressure as he confides to me what he
    was dreaming ..."

&

"The limpid liquid within the young man ..."

"What a queen!" I think,
remembering how naïve & surprised I was to find out he was gay,
though certainly not as surprised as when I found out my father was.

I wish Whitman could have saved him—
streaking back across the dark skies of history in his hot pink tights
with that grassy "WW" emblazoned across his chest
to kiss his eyes & tell him he would be alright.

I snap the book shut after a few pages,
head back to the kitchen for a drink of cold water
& stand in front of the window fan in my boxer shorts,
hand on my hip,
staring out at Whitman's city—
all the night's lights winking at me.

When God Created Pigeons

When God created pigeons he probably thought:
Man needs a flying crap vacuum
as he reached down into his big bag of rocks
& took his Bubblicious bubblegum out of his mouth
and made two little feet.
Then he waved his magic wand over his creation,
said something in Pig Latin
and sprinkled a little bit of fairy dust on it
to give it wings, which is why their feathers are iridescent
in the late June light at Soho park
where I eat my lunch
and watch a hostile mob of them
peck at each other's faces
and hobble around on their little stumps of bubblegum
as they vie for their big chance at the giant hunk
of stale bagel.

I've always preferred to think of God as a flamboyant magician
twisting his waxy black moustache
as he doffs his top hat
from which he just pulled a platypus
to impress his only begotten son.

"I will go down to the people and show them these magical tricks and
    illusions,
and they will believe in you!"
said the son to his father, for he was bored and lonely.

"No, son ... wait!"
But it was too late.

And so it was that Jesus came down to earth
And walked on water

And turned water to wine
And multiplied fish
And healed the sick
And fed the poor
And raised the dead
And died
And rose again
Just like David Blaine

Toothpick Eyeballs

"The Truth Is Right Here,"
says the little plastic box of tea tree toothpicks
as I stare at the odd polish on the rounded ends of their little handles
all bunched together like a bundle of tiny Marty Feldman eyeballs.

"Even in a box of well-polished Tea tree toothipicks?" I ask it,
glum about my prospects
of ever having a moment to write here in New York
where my mind feels splattered out across the city
like Walt Whitman's brain on the floor of the American Anthropometric
    Society,
where it was removed for phrenological analysis
and subsequently dropped by a careless assistant
who I picture as Marty Feldman playing Igor in *Young Frankenstein*
when the glass jar of genius shatters at his feet
& my roommate interrupts me to tell me about the Olafur Eliasson
    waterfalls,
which pump water up from the East River through a mass of scaffolding
& splatter it back out across the East River.

At the End of the World

I used to be more preoccupied with death,
though I now seem to be more concerned with why life can't be more
    beautiful more of the time,
particularly when our time here is so brief, I think
as I stand at the corner of Houston & Varick
waiting for my wife and son to pop out of the subway like gophers—
gophers on the way to see the new Herzog documentary about Antarctica.

You hardly ever hear about gophers in poems these days
as they stand above their dark holes
& scout about anxiously for their families beneath the marquee of the
    Gopher-Plex,
waiting to see the new documentary about a misanthropic gopher who
    has traveled to Antarctica
to show us both the pathos & the beauty in the absurd clash of gopher
    culture, science & nature on the world's most inhospitable continent.
It was a good movie, though flawed, & left me wishing it had been
    distilled into a more perfect beauty, though where would the truth in
    that be?
Which is how I feel about this poem
about a misanthropic man who has traveled to New York City
to show us both the pathos & beauty in the absurd clash of family, time
    & death in the world's most inhospitable city
before he looks away from the bright, incomprehensible world
& returns to his dark hole.

Brighton Beach Nocturne
—for Aaron Eastburn

I'd like to make out with David Bowie on the cover of *Hunky Dory*
with his goldilocks pulled back from his face with that practiced look of
    fashion agony,
& go to Brighton Beach on the Q train
& eat various sausages from King's Meats
as the airplanes on the horizon drag banners for the Boy George concert
    at Terminal 5 on the 14TH.
"He stole it all from me," he'll say & wink & give me that dogtooth sneer.
"Karma Chameoleon … twat."
Then we'll giggle & roll around on our Mexican blanket & smoke
    Liggets & drink Tall Boys
& admire the fat old Polish tranny in the neon bikini,
& beg the muscle-bound closet cases
to come kick sand in our faces
until the sun goes down on the Hudson
& the pixilated skyline goes flat
before the screen goes black.

Another Poem

The mysteries of the universe are contained
in a single varicose vein. Funny thing
about language that things that sound true
sound true as all the ideas in Manhattan
blow down the avenues like not-that-beautiful
leaves—interesting, maybe, but not useful where
the greater indifference of the universe is concerned.

"God wouldn't have invented varicose veins or the indifference of the
        universe if he didn't find them interesting,"
says the fat man in the stained, baby-blue New York Sanitation
        Department T-shirt to himself
as he sweeps the leaves into little piles at the base of the camouflage trees
with his mighty broom like Hercules
in one last heroic act of futility against monotheism
here in this little park
before the breeze scatters them all about
and they make this grating scraping sound across the bricks,
wishing they were ideas instead of similes.

Art Out of the Present

"The hardest thing is to make art out of the present,"
said an artist to me
many years ago in San Francsico
as he pointed to a Newport menthol billboard & raised his eyebrows.
I made a collage for him in a little matchbox that had the outline of a
    couple having sex in the missionary position
floating in front of the black-and-hospital-green daggers of a Newport
    menthol box I later picked up on the street.
I gave it to him, but he never said anything,
which led me to believe the more compelling truth:
The hardest thing is to get anyone to give a shit about anything—
these poorly installed, fake parquet floors, for example,
here beneath my feet in this apartment in Brooklyn,
unimportant, yet making an impression upon my mind,
which wishes it were thinking about something else more weighty &
    important
like love or death in uncliché terms that carry time itself
in a blue metal Brooklyn basket
like the one right next to my desk
with our laundry in it,
which I need to fold & put away.

On the Staten Island Ferry

I can almost see Spalding Gray's face,
red flannel shirt, black jeans & knee brace
receding beneath the graphite Vija Celmins waves
as he jumps from this boat crossing this river
to another boat crossing another river.

"Looks like spit," my son says.
"I'm gonna spit in it."
Then he spits in it.

How to Become a Scrub Jay

Death, stay behind me
perched on the windowsill next to the John Deere tractor.
You can't hear the airplanes flying overhead on their way to LaGuardia
or the sloshing sound of air conditioners in the light well
because you are just a Mexican wooden carving of a skeleton
my friend Daniel gave to me in San Francisco many years ago
when he moved out of that garden apartment near Dolores Park
where Carl tried out getting his dick sucked by this really annoying bald
    guy named Tom.
"Well, you could do better than *that*," I said when he complained that he
    couldn't sport one.
Death also doesn't have to go to work today, or fret about whether his
    writing is any good
while wasting his time thinking about a man who wishes he were a
    Scrub Jay with a beautiful voice instead of that hideous squawk they
    make,
nevermind how to become a Scrub Jay.

Poem on My 36TH Birthday

I wonder if I ride my bike through Brooklyn fast enough
if the particles of Walt Whitman
would smash into my face
revealing the mysteries of the universe,
which means what—one singing or one seeing?
"Universe," I mean.
Maybe that is the mystery: one song and ...
Is that what the universe is—
an incredibly mysterious and incomprehensibly beautiful song
like the verse of Walt Whitman
in which his particles almost certainly still live
and still sing from the letters strung out
into words and lines, etc., like secret codes
that smash into your brain and open up
alternate dimensions
like little fireworks of joy and sadness
that are actually galaxies
standing in the grass at Prospect Park
playing with a planet earth beach ball
beneath the fried chicken clouds
with my son, my wife.
36 years old.

USELYSSES

Aubade

I love to ride my bicycle to work
beneath the gauntlet of bare-knuckle spring elms …
But isn't a gauntlet also a glove?
Bare-knuckle gloves, hmpff …

Well, I like my bicycle ride anyway—
the early birds programming their computers up in the tree tops
beneath the OK sky. It's OK
for things to be OK
rather than great or horrible—
"great" *being* horrible, in fact, because you know your cardboard heart,
which shoots off into space at a 45 degree angle,
will soon do so in a line without an angle
as its relationship to everything becomes, well, complicated
like an arrow of thermodynamics
that *can* be destroyed
when it goes "poof" in the hydrogen flames of a distant, angry sun …
Sad, actually, that it isn't part of a better-respected constellation
after all these years of burning with such diligence
out there in the otherwise dark.

Years … What are years to a sun
like the one toward which
the bald head of this earth
now nods with its cirrus combover?
So obvious & beautiful
this morning
in this boring
mid-size, middle-American City.

Ballad of the Homeopathic Pony

"A Homeopathic Pony," says the message from outer space,
which arrives on a homeopathic pony from a distant planet
billions of light years away. It has arrived here instantaneously
through a space travel method known as "crumpling"
in which the universe is simply balled up into a wad of simultaneity
by the invisible hands of the unknowable god
for the universe is but a sheet of paper
on which god has written the words "A Homeopathic Pony"
for reasons that not even he can explain
& crumpled it up in disgust.
But now it exists: a homeopathic pony
as you uncrumple the message and behold the mighty steed
here to save us all from minor ailments & skin irritations,
disease, greed, evil, this
soul-crushing depression, etc ...

They Say You Need a Slogan for Christmas
—for Mia, Nico & Lucy

"They say you need a slogan for Christmas,"
says my son at dinner,
blowing the steam from the dumpling in his split pea soup.
"Mine's going to be 'Destruction!'" he declares.
Then he sets his spoon down
and blows up a red balloon.
"Look, Dad—Perfume!" he says
puffing his neck with his own breath
from the red latex nozzle.

But I'm still thinking about who "they" are—
they who might have adamantly suggested to my son
that Christmas requires a personal slogan
as my mind drifts through the ages from space
scouring the dark continents of yore
for the origin and history of this statement—
tracing it backward through a genealogy of all language
like a map of lightning
that disappears into the William Blake clouds
where God, compass and protractor in hand,
looks down upon his own son from on high
as he leans in toward the manger
with Wizard's hair and Whitman's beard
and whispers in his ear:
"Destruction!"

Behind This Groucho Marx Disguise

Behind this Groucho Marx disguise
lies a face made of fruits
like Arcimboldo vs. Carmen Miranda
with a manly banana jawline that …
squeaks?
     Rusty because I hardly write
poems anymore, not that I have anything
against them, but they can't possibly make
sense of this world, only a sliver of which I
can't even begin to describe
as I look out through this open door,
which frames our garden in a trapezoid:
sunflowers and rainbow chard with cabbage moths,
Russian sage and iris blades staving off the weeds
like Arcimboldo got beat up
in the Garden of Good and Evil.

"Gertrude Stein was the Nostradamus of the dance remix!"
I suddenly realize
as a cloud of diesel smoke rises from the garbage truck in the alley
like the evil specter of "So what?"
then makes its escape through the elm branches
into the clear blue Colorado sky.

Some Mornings I Wake Up

Some mornings I wake up
having completely forgotten that I'm a magical wizard
as I shuffle about in the kitchen making coffee
and stirring the wet food
into the dry food
as though life were something ordinary
and the mystic song of the dog food in this stainless steel bowl
were nothing more or less than the mashing sound of nasty meat.

"Heeeeerrrrrre Yggdrasil!" I call to my dragon
remembering now
as he bounds across the castle floor
& wags his pointy tail
like an ordinary dog who loves dog food.

I don't know why my dragon loves dog food,
but I'm happy he's happy
and happy he's reminded me
that it's the small things in this life that matter.

Then I hug my son & kiss my wife
for I must ride to meet the dawn.
The Army of Darkness has gathered in the East,
and I must carve my name upon the tree of life.

American Dreams

1.

Biggie Smalls

nesting dolls

2.
—*for Chris Selvig*

We met up with you and Ruby and Lula at some sand dunes where there
were Dune Sharks swimming with bears in the sand and you seemed
OK with the kids playing with them, so I was OK with it. Then you
gave me a rare book that had an essay in it about Björk by Richard Hell.
It also had a pink vinyl record in the shape of a splash that played a
scratchy sepia documentary about Nicholas Cage's early career (his real
last name was Lug) as a clerk in a hardware store. Later in the dream
we arrived at a meadow with a muddy pond and I realized I'd gone the
wrong way. A wizard who looked like Gargamel came out and said, "I
told you not to go the wrong way!" and I said, "Well, we were on our way
to see you, so what does it matter?" and he just shrugged.

3.

Someone I dislike immensely
asks me if I will introduce *Psycho* at a screening
& and I say, "Why not?" matter-of-factly
though I'm not sure why since I can't stand him.

Then, just before the lights go down, I'm prompted
to get up in front of my seat & explain
that it was the first true Western with the possible exception of
    The Searchers.

"Hitchcock asks us to forgive the villains,"
I say to the audience of well-meaning dip-shits,
"who've been neutered into crimes of the unconscious
by the lonely horror of the landscape itself
& the violent schizophrenia that lies between memory & dreams."

Their faces glaze over so I cut myself short,
tell them to read *Blood Meridian*,
then go backstage & do my thinning frightwig up like Lion-O's from
    Thundercats
to get ready for my interview with George W. Bush who,
stupid as he may pretend be,
knows the truth as well as I.

Prepared for Peace
—for Marc Huebert

There's a bear in the woods.
For some people, the bear is easy to see.
Others: don't see it at all.
Some people say the bear is tame;
others say it's vicious and dangerous.
Since no one can really be sure who's right,
isn't it smart to be as strong as the bear
if there is a bear?

God Wasn't Dead

God wasn't dead, though
it is true that after his novel became a best-seller
he moved to a small town in New Hampshire
& raised Bantam chickens
after his only son became a cult leader
& threatened to disclose his home address
to the throngs of his disenchanted fans
who wanted a sequel.

"Here, you write it," he finally said to his son
one snowy Xmas Eve
and gave him the outline
& a few rough character sketches
for a past-future, sci-fi satire
"… about a world of illiterate people who worship books.
But all bets are off when an exiled clan of homosexual aliens
secretly raise an orphaned boy
& teach him how to read & write.
The Keeper of the Books will stop at nothing to destroy him
before he writes a new prophecy
& the people discover … *The Messiah*."

"I was thinking *Life of Brian* meets *Beyond the Valley of the Dolls*,
but maybe pitch it as conceptual memoir?"
he called out to his only son whom he loved so dearly
one last time through the driving white blizzard of asterisks.

"Sure thing, Dad!" he said, and gave the thumbs up
as he scraped the snow off his Subaru.

When Physicists Finally Discover Irreducible Matter

When physicists finally discover irreducible matter,
it will not be strings, but letters—
The Alphabet of God
written upon the paper of the Universe.

"Well, what does it say!?" demands one of the scientists,
turning to his colleagues
who stand before the truth in their white lab coats
like pillars of salt in the desert of questions.

"Everything!" I shout to them from the past
and then:

"Everything!" a voice booms in the room around them.

And they tremble before my voice,
which they have mistaken for God's.

Knock Knock, I bang on the door.

"Who's there?" they say,
cowering behind the collider.

"Multiple choice question," I answer
because it's so obvious that it's all been written
in the choose-you-own-adventure of Time.

"Multiple choice question who?"
they ask from behind the door
between the past and the future,
but I can't think of a punch line.

Grape Iris

The computer program in the grape iris says:
If gauntlet of floppy hospital green swords in mid-April,
then preposterous lilac vagina with rabbit ears that smells like grapes.
And thusly does beauty triumph over life & its myriad attendant horrors
for a too-short moment in Spring
before my mind frowns down upon it all from some dumb height
because it cannot understand a goddamn thing about it.

I Used to Get Lost in the Saying

I used to get lost in the saying
"A stitch in time saves 9"
as though it were the headline for a story
about the 9 Mysterious Lords of the Universe
imperiled by a scissor-clawed beast
snipping away at the very woof of space-time
from the terrifying realm beyond infinity
where the unknowable pounces on form to destroy it.

"All would surely have been lost
but for the sartorial heroics of the thimble-fingered 9
shrouded in their cloaks of midnight,
gallantly guarding the fragile fabric of our benevolent reality!"
went the final line in the report
which rang out in the stentorian voice of Orson Welles
as we raised our glasses of Paul Masson
to toast their triumph over The Formless.

And so it was I wasted my youth.

Thou Art My Dearest Deer

"Thou art my dearest dear,"
the agent whispers in my ear
then slips a fortune cookie in my pocket.

"Things as they are," it says,
so I wander my face for years
asleep in the cipher of memory:

a dildo in a rollerskate;
a basket full of buttons;
dog barf on the baby blue shag rug;
the trap door in my mother's closet;
1513 N. Nevada Avenue;
colored condom balloons covered in cat hair;
my little yellow wicker rocking chair ...

"Loneliness made me stupid,"
I confess to my muse, unable to crack the code.
She has gorgeous tits and a winning smile
though I find myself distracted by her baby blue ball cap that says:
"DREAMS" in puffy rainbow letters across the front.

I want to fuck her so bad, but she says let's wait.
"Everything's almost exactly as it seems," she reassures me.

"Thou are my dearest deer,"
I whisper in her ear
still lost in the misunderstanding
though I think I know exactly what she means.

Insect Dust

I was at the high school riot
hiding in the bathroom stall
& the arugula grew tall
& you held up a bumper crop of cars
as you sashayed through Shanghai
with a sheep's worth of hair

This, my dream,
only dimly remembered
over grapefruit & bacon—
such a light and pleasant adventure
to push around on paper here
as Plato blathers on about the allegory,
tracing it with his laser pointer

"Put a cork in it," I mutter under my breath from the back of the cave
& try to lift the boulder of my dream to crush him.

But it's too heavy.

Perhaps I will try to lift it later.

I crumble a dead insect
onto this piece of paper instead
where it sits at the top of this poem
as though it were the title,

as though

I wished this poem were a different poem—
the poem I meant to write
about the molecules of water that touched the hooves of Caesar's pony

as he reared up and hollered "Hi Ho, Silver!"
in the middle of the Rubicon.

But it's too late, &
this is this poem,
y'know?

Once Upon a Time

I woke up too early, but felt happy to have coffee in bed & stare at the red, blue & turquoise cross-stitch flowers on our filthy quilt.

Went to a few yard sales, bought a sleeping bag & a rubber mallet, a saw, a prybar, & a blue backpack for $10.

Took photos of some old car-shaped opaque glass cologne bottles & a folder with a wolf on it at another yard sale.

Came home.

Big Bell Magazine arrived in the mail from Jason Morris in San Francisco. Beautiful.

Ate a delicious curry chicken salad over a bed of lightly braised red potatoes, wax beans & arugula from our garden that Marina made.

Took *Big Bell Magazine* to bed to see what the poets in San Francisco are up to.

Took a nap.

Sarah came by with her fat new terrier & a creepy plate with an expressionless girl in a purple dress on a blue chair holding a doll she picked up at the Episcopal Thrift House. At first she said she paid 50 cents for it, but then she admitted it was in the free box.

Got dressed.

Took Ursen to gymnastics.

Talked on the phone with Daniel in Denver for a few minutes, but he kept cutting out.

Got in an argument with a guy on a beach cruiser who almost ran over us. He said he would "smack me in my fucking face like a little bitch" when I told him to watch where he was going as we walked down the alley to a party for refugees at Lutheran Family Services where Aaron works.

Ate Iraqi chicken, drank chai & watched the Nepalis dance in their pretty colored hats.

Picked up a couple sodas & two limes at Mountain Mama for movie night.

Picked up lemons & rosemary at King Soopers.

Listened to the XX with Ursen in the car out in front of The Arc.

Listened to a report on how the oil spill is affecting the birds in the gulf.

Came home, took off my pants & opened the windows.

Listened to Ursen read a few Calvin & Hobbes strips.

Went outside to tell the dogs to stop barking when the neighbor whispered from her kitchen window, "There's four deer in Butch's yard."

Sat down on the porch in my boxer shorts & watched them nibble on the elm leaves until they spooked & disappeared around the corner.

Ouroboros
—for Kevin Opstedal

"Is it corny to believe in magic?" I wonder,
as the afternoon light hits the filthy silver garbage can
casting a beautiful donut of rope angels onto my kitchen floor.

"Well I can tell you that I don't believe in angels,
 though a man should never phheressenpfeffer,
if you ask me, for such sertionschleppers certainly assenbaffer!"
I think, as I stare at the halo—aware as I say it
that such assertions of certainty are for jerks—
jerks who can't face the terrifying magic of unknowing
toward which we must cast ourselves
headlong into the future—
detaching our very heads
from our bodies like bowling balls
to roll them down the long lane of fate toward the ...

THUNK

only to be swallowed by the terrifying machinery of eternal
return. Whooop! My head magically pops up through the garbage can,
thinking about a metaphysical donut.

Vija Celmins & The Case of the Nocturnal Pocketbook
—for Darin Klein & Owen Hill

I wish I were reading a mystery called
Vija Celmins & The Case of the Nocturnal Pocketbook
in which an insensitive amateur detective named Abner Badminton
gets hired to uncover the mystery behind *Time Magazine* art critic
    Richard Lacayo's statement:
"[Celmins'] 'all over' images of desert floors, outer space or the ocean
    surface, their apparent uniformity is built from a superabundance of
    subdued visual incidents,"
which he traces to a blog post dated Monday, March 19, 2007 at 12:02 P.M.

The whole case hinges on the impenetrable "superabundance of subdued
    visual incidents"
as we follow Badminton through the usual ruses, twists & turns—
trysts with slide librarians & the like,
until he discovers the obvious, which is that it doesn't really mean
    anything at all
beyond sort of sounding good.

"The real mystery is the mysterious beauty of the drawings of Vija Celmins!"
declares Badminton at the reveal with an uncharacteristic exuberance
(obviously softened by his encounters with Celmins' flattened vastnesses)
as a nervous silence befalls his patrons.

"And what of the nocturnal pocketbook?" asks Margaret—
the wanton heiress—as she pinches her smoke-stained ivory quellazaire
between the white-gloved thumb & index finger of her left hand
& stabs at her mother's pearls with the right in a gesture that says
    nothing if not:
All loose ends *must* be tidied.
"Well, it just ..." Badminton stammers for effect,
& only furtively reciprocates Margaret's gaze.
"It just sounds good!" he says.
And everyone agrees it just sounds good.

Poem

What does it mean that I saw a Montana-shaped cloud
flexing its Arm & Hammer bicep
above the west side Walgreens
Mid-July, 2009?

Not much, I fear,
wishing I felt something other than this sadness
which billows through me sort of like the breeze that blows
through my window, barely puffing up the curtains
like sails on a ship that's sailing into itself,
like one of those weird tube snakes
or a boat that's also a black hole with a stage
on which friends and enemies act out
scenes without a plot,
but cannot stay
(the curtains close; you read their obituaries in the paper the next day).

Sadly, you are always a member of the audience—
dismayed at the flimsy metaphor
collapsing into the black hole
as you curse the universe and toss your newspaper
into the internet.

The stage turns inside out
into a day without a frame
with a big bright sun that's so obviously God
sending his rays through space
to save us from the meaningless arm of Montana
& touch our faces.

Nothing Always Happens

Love's true bluish line
divides space from time—
moments kindly separated from measure
(*pssst*: You get to keep the secret treasure)
in your pirate's chest
with a magic latch
& bury it inside your breast.

Then line by line
you make a map,
but then go blind
& have to get a double eye patch
& spend your days trying to find
your treasure in the sands of time,
wondering how you became a pirate?
when all you really wanted to be
was a 19ᵀᴴ Century whaling narrative
full of nautical & cetaceous terms like
mizzen-mast & ambergris,
butterbox galliots, bilocular hearts
& long lays.

Championship Champagne Bologna
—for Craig Richardson

"This here's Championship Champagne Bologna country!"
you said on your useless hill outside Hartsel,
and we knew it was true.

I kicked over some cowshit,
then we got into a hybrid vehicle
and ran over the log.

Because I am a poet
my soul is a filthy mirror.

Some people mistake it for a window
and think they can see through me.

But all they really see is the truth of their own hearts
Reflected in my dirty art.

You know what I mean.
And we sang it all the way back down to Colorado Springs:

Championship Champagne Bologna!
It's the *champagne* of Bolognas.
(Now available in powder packets.)

Poem of Carl Sagan

It must be confusing for Christians
who arrive in Heaven
to find Carl Sagan seated at the right hand of God,
which is a gigantic, glowing vagina
floating above the Captain's chair
on the deck of the Starship Enterprise.

"It's interesting—and I never imagined this—"
says Carl, using the weirding voice of Science to soothe the recently dead,
"that the Universe is merely an emanation of the brain,
which, as we look into it, tricks us into believing
that we are gazing into an unfathomable outward expanse
that is but the unknowable inner reaches of our own minds. Now,
who would like to be reborn?"

Hands shoot up among the small crowd of Christians
as the vagina opens to reveal a wormhole
outlined in a grid of astral light.

"Courbet was right!" says Carl, winking at the crowd.

"But why are we on the Starship Enterprise?" asks C.S. Lewis,
visibly confounded by the inferno of truth before him.
"And where's the Holy Ghost?"

"The Starship Enterprise *is* the Holy Ghost,"
Sagan says with a smile of pure benevolence.
"Only death can carry us to the stars,
which is only another way of saying that the spirit is a time machine,"
he adds, his Spock-like eyebrows cresting.
"Read *Dune* again—it explains everything."

Then he unzips his burnt-orange windbreaker
and a laser of love shoots out

from the spectral Starfleet logo upon his heart,
zapping them all into a rapture of wordless knowledge
as God folds their souls into dream.

Praise for Penis Jonson

"… and those who would censor or silence themselves or others to protect
the imagined sensibilities of those who would sacrifice truth for morality
shalt dwell forever in the realm of the unsung fuckface!"
proclaims Penis Jonson
in his valedictory speech
at the Xanadu Beauty School graduation
as the grass, long gone to seed, goes wild.
Then the topiary lummox rises from the garden of good & evil
and yawns into the snappy flat blue sky.
"With great freedom comes great indifference," he whispers.
"Say whatever you want; no one gives a shit—
this is poetry!
Make a list of birds you've seen this Spring,
rename them things like Fernando Valenzuela,
then decide it was a waste of time.
However, know this: The Great Rainbow Snake will swallow
hideous truths and beautiful lies indiscriminately.
In either case, only The Great Rainbow Snake will remain.
Then, eventually, it, too, will die …
Do you understand?"
Penis Jonson nods, then looks down at his brown socks and starts to cry.
"Cheer up! Your son will find a bloody rabbit's foot near a patch of snow
in a nearby canyon and place it on the bookshelf next to the stapler."
He smiles.
You sigh.
Then: "Congratulations!" he says
and hands you your diploma.

Sausage Ice

"Sausage Ice ..."
You subvocalize it, careful not to say it too loudly
because you never thought you'd say such a thing,
nevermind its actual existence.

But there it is—scattered on the counter
like a tiny replica of the Fortress of Solitude
made from meat crystals
as you chip the frozen sausages apart
and put them in the pan with a little oil,
then run a bath & rouse your son for school.

You don't know it now,
but later this morning you'll come home & wash greasy Christmas lights
    in a bowl full of warm soapy water.
Also: a black cat will sit in front of your studio door, which has a
    Canadian flag on it that your wife painted in Halloween colors.
And you'll think about:
Gayle Ferrel & Dick Dale singing "One Toke Over the Line" on the *The*
    Lawrence Welk Show,
which you saw on YouTube last week,
& which struck you as something truly spiritual in its absurdity;
& all the people who killed themselves this year;
& your friends who don't call or write much anymore,
& vice versa.

Uselysses

My two favorite movies are probably …
Fitzcarraldo & *The Swimmer*
starring Klaus Kinski & Burt Lancaster respectively
& both of which I realize now, as I write this,
are about deranged, yet well-intentioned men
who embark upon journeys of beautiful uselessness,
which sounds like Uselysses—
the hero of this poem
about a man who comes home from work
& takes a bath.

If I were that man,
I would be 1/64TH my actual size
so that I could swim across my bathtub
in my tiny little Speedo
then haul my son's little wooden boat
up over the giant pile of dirty laundry at the foot of our bed
& sail it toward the fjords
in the photo above the toilet
& smash into the glass
because pointlessness is beauty.

MOBY K. DICK

Moby K. Dick

Uncertain, fugitive, half-fabulous, American
we took their word to determine our own

The blank insanity of Ahab, ere the white whale:
a sheet of onionskin paper blurred third or fourth carbon

And this brought about new revelations—
stolen libraries of earth spilling fiction by autorocket

Do you see that queer fashion where fluke minds the tongue
like an Android brain humming to say from beyond

"The sperm would have you forming yourself"
to all who had fused; you owe it to them.

Not the less true to be recorded
in the empathy box.

Lord Jim Thompson

When the truth aims at facts—Lo, I call no one to explain anything.
You think: My God—there's no way of telling.
I tell you: The truth involves innumerable shakes of obscure cheroot
    bullied into phantoms of the inconceivable—
supersonic, jet-propelled, propeller-driven dicks of truth trepanning the
    subconscious.
Believe me, I'd like to know something besides pay.
It's as easy as nothing to do, only much better,
dismounting the butterfly with a stentorian voice stolen from
    misanthropic books
in one square aperture of nonsense built with opulent black glitter of
    deception on the unqualified lawn.
"The kid seemed quite contented hustling wood in Hell," they said.
"But he was one of us, and that's the end."
The story had run out and we need another.

Paul Austerlitz

As a young boy I fell into the classic snow & built a cash register to
    speak the language of life.
And so it was the ruins of form cast a whole underworld beneath a
    rainbow.
It gradually dawned on me that I was an embarrassing document.
I wish now I could have vanished, father. I wish I could feel through the
    green meadows at the headstreams of the Dwy Fawr & Dwy Fach.
The only thing I wanted was to write the person I thought I was
but I could never say, drifting through a faded squadron of faces.
Every piece of paper I touched sparkled into a hundred & fifty people
until the great throng suddenly shut up
& the labyrinths were born
time in one hand, money in the other
as if the words before me were a small boy speaking the mask.

Watchmen in the Rye

Nobody cares I've spent eight years running around in a costume of
good & evil like a dirty stupid sonuvabitch of a moron

as I come to understand the madness Blake revealed, my father's death—
the fascinating story of your goddam life, that's all (I damn near puked).

Manhattan: I made a mistake. Some super-duper nostalgia where once
    we all lived for our sentence.
Boy I felt miserable—like atheist Jesus with a lot of makeup. I felt so
    depressed you can't imagine.

Went to retrieve my face and became myself.
You can rent those, darling. I really did look damn good in it, too.

You want to know what's behind this corpse, flapping dismally beneath
    my dreams?
She wasn't too sexy or anything, but even so you can't help wondering.

We'd been blasted to fragments in the helpless silence.
She has about five thousand notebooks.

Queer as a goon with a necklace of heads,
all I said was English was my best subject.

Best tell your superiors that I'm leaving—
Arizona first, I think, then Mars.

Huckleberry Finnegans Wake

Who is I? Well you answer me dis
What matter creature ought to be leashed under the mysttetry?
By and by everybody hears a horse a-comin on t'other side of the river
Crossing it is surely the signature of a better bargain
I've only got one memory: Hamlet's yawn—
a song to be cutting up with a pair of sissers
It ain't no name for it leastways I kinder forget
the dream monologue traversing days not worth remembering,
my mind a woody dark. All right, I'll got to hell
in those good old lousy days gone by—
I've got a rope ladder and a pen, some common blood.

Male & female we unmask the ghoon to an inch of his core
& I warn't myself as I opened the door.

Past now pulls the pit for limericks—
I'll tell you the way to Mars:
pass through grass alone, last loved, end here.

The Spy Who Came in from the Cold Blood

The impossible task of identifying a personality from the incomplete
    records
to usurp space allotted to the future with a different tinted ink written in
    three styles of script.

Whatever motives he had were concealed beneath a cloak of papers.
People talked a murmuring cave of speculation without confession.

The truth is this: memory could scarcely be bothered; intelligence was
    the enemy.
His pen raced in pursuit of the narrative—a tale of petty thievery.

"I hate it, but it's a tiny price for the ordinary rain pattering on the roof,
    the sky lit with dingy streetlights."
He shows a pattern of feeling through antisocial dreams, a tendency to
    form other people:
vain fools, traitors, pansies, sadists, drunkards, monks ... cowboys,
    Indians—

faces painting self-portraits spilled halfway across the smashed light
bursting in upon them with meaning as though the detective discovered
    himself,
empty & worthless.

The Thief's Journals of Lewis & Clark

Should I have to portray a convict lovingly doomed to organize a forbidden
    language
across the ravages of these United States—a messenger amiss with fear
beneath the shabby skyes, I was to walk the amputated shores
below the mouth built in this form with a glass of whiskey.

At times I would wander the city, haggle the orgy of moral lines whose
    heroes I've wanted to live
(considerable anxiety with respect to the snake notwithstanding)
with the vilest words to swipe the conquered furniture,
these savages of merchandise who took down the language.

A distinguished poet helps me ransack the rooms of legend, reading my
    life in other words.
We have made up our minds on our homeward journey
by inventing heroic acts, the appearances of honor peculiar to hoodlums.

All arrangements now compleated, I took leave of myself from the
    opposite shore
to live again with my mouth open for the theft & thieves,
our country, our politicks, & our friends.

Notes from Under the Volcano

I was ashamed that I would never turn into a different person.

At 29, still dreamed, even then, of changing the world through dreams:

A palace of breasts, for example, need only be a pleasure and won't be
boring

having so magnificently abandoned the Puritans.

My colleagues seemed to look at my pockmarked face with a certain
embarrassed loathing.

"Why goodness me …," "What a delightful surprise …,"—one could not
imagine success.

Then the spell of little debauches I'd reconciled to "everything beautiful
& lofty" bore no resemblance to either hero or mud.

Listening to the babel across the years, I picked up a paperback &
opened it with a sigh.

The strange truth was beautiful like the spectral mole of a great dark
garbage.

Quite lost in my ragged old poetry, I hissed to be born somehow from an
idea.

It was the game that fascinated me most of all.

Remembrance of the Amnesiac

He had brought to such a horror of vulgarity the fine art of concealment
of aesthetically precious personal allusion in a wealth of ingenious
circumlocution

The missing part of his heart still only a fragment he wrote down in his
black notebook at the border of remembrance.

Sometimes a spell would rise inscribed with an immensity of visionary
longings—ashamed & wretched as though torn from his own head

weather in the memory—the autumn grayness, stale vestiges of a limbo
between chapters in other words, dazzling black box, & a desk by
the window

So it was that figures of speech named strangers in his hearing to
furnish him with explanations for those dreams of the memory

Only a vague room of papers nostalgic for the present

"It's alright," he said, languishing at the brink. "I think, though, that this
one isn't quite straight."

Afterwards, he listened to all the friends who had died or been
hospitalized in the last year guffaw a strange mocking

as happens at times to people suffering a case of the most ordinary words.

Slaughterhouse 2666

When I was younger I was a writer
protected by the fourth dimension
in whom mysteries spontaneously talked
a scrambled pattern,
which I will write later on.

One of them will be two books
mentally unsettling the landscape
with the branches of science fiction.

Somewhere in there was an awful disgust
calling like Roland for memories
to dig new pits for the disappeared.

One morning I was leading a happy life
& let the snow fall
& read the futurists with love and nostalgia—
backwards and forwards in the moment blob
to hide cleverly inside voice boxes
& never hurt again.

People so often read a few pages of my book
without peering into the strange forest of words around the boring city.
The fairy hero in there with all those knives
cut up my friends in little pieces.

Pure blather emerges unscathed—the sound of utter silence
pretending to read
from the bodies who talked & fucked in ideologies.

Me, I'm a young idiot with hundreds of rotten tombstones for a brain
who flunked out of heart and the nature of time.

Allow me to introduce no one.
No one remembers the writer.
He tore himself to pieces
for a new technique.

Pinocchiorwell

A fine spelling book in my little brain, tomorrow I will begin to write
    and earn a great deal of money—
riches more than minds can picture, teaching the beasts by song
so as to arrive at the field of miracles by morning, and rest from our
    sweet suffering—
no work besides reading & writing & the afternoons given up to
    recreation.

Oh, but they want to rob me of my time—infamous villains!—in what
    world we are condemned
to mingle with the animals & teach them the tune of the permanently bad
    terms of their own interests.

"Open up your mouth & deliver the money or you are dead."
"Pigs now sleep in cryptic remarks," I utter with a cry of despair, the
    first victory of a nailed mouth.

The attack came and the animals pronounced the death of the impossible
as desperation began to eat the word for tomorrow
& then a scene happened that would seem impossible if it were not true:
    recitations of poems
& the animals walked round and round their masterpiece

Farenheit 49

Something lay hidden behind the face like a clock in a mausoleum
as if death drew blood against the futureless breath of somebody else's life.

"I'll show you my collection of time someday," he tried to conjure
but the sign depicted the face of an everchanging payday.

"There you have it, you can stay happy all the time—read comics at
    funerals,"
she said, a little desperate, & looked around for the name of god with her
    teeth.

A squirrel stood looking at *The Bible* in the shut up silence
like a homosexual about to fall in love.

He remembered the books that had no name or identity & tried to piece
    it all together
in a normal pattern of life—a generic walking assembly of man.

They stood by the luminous dial of his watch with verse in their heads
at the end of the Holy Roman Empire amid the splendid delusions of
    paranoia

shouting the sound of death into every blade of grass—
Americans speaking their language by accident.

Miss Lonelyhearts of Darkness
—for Richard Hell & Will Yackulic

His face was a trick in a bookstore, a fist in this jungle of adding
    machines, a small amount of money called the soul.
To face the darkness, the yarns of regret, the powerless disgust, he was
    cheered by keeping his eye on chance.
He felt better knowing himself a faker & a fool, a love story out of a
    garbage can feeling the guilt of torn mouths
becoming neither god nor devil, let alone letters from dictation.
The rest of his outfit didn't go well with a thick billfold.
He looked incomplete—a frightful gash, shoes full of blood, one hand
    from the woods illuminating the last hope on earth.
"Come, tell us, priests of cripple hearts, how it was that you first came to
    believe in jokes," he muttered.
He had no opinion but shrugs—like a mask of interrupted phrases
    ending in appalled dumbness.

He could not destroy his teeth without dreaming a large batch of letters.
Nothing will remain but a light sigh.

Fredrick X-Men
—for Kit Bland

I remember feeling the uneasiness of myself
appearing as though by magic, the unseen mutant.

My illness: America; I was much given to fantasy.
My costumed youths attacking me as foe,

I took table with skeptics in the library, was tired,
for I am indeed one of those destined to steal

a novel of transitional thoughts dealt only in symbolic essences.
Like the great epics, our book-length thriller begins:

"I will live my life a lesser man, a poet—
a muscle-bound bookworm in the silent chamber of invisible eyes."

The unwriting writer vigorously lathering my genitalia & yodeling
The Waste Land to protect mankind.

Pierre Menard, Author of The Capote
—in memory of Ron Miller

The visible works left behind by the late lamented poet:
long, wrinkled white linen breeches, a girlish tenderness, red dust, a
    moustache,
a sentimental poetic vocabulary for the suppression of reality,
a clump of goldenrod to summon a monkey.

This work, possibly the most significant of our time, consists of
    everything,
but a lot prettier and on an island of dreams.

The initial method he conceived being chance autobiography of another
    personage
in a wheedling singsong of reiterated grievances.

Imagine the universe is an accidental book
as though the stars wrote out their dreams in the dark watching
Poe, Baudelaire, Mallarmé, Valéry …

They would need this magic of the cloud hotel
swept along by variants of the the "original" text.

God lay unclothed in space, all undefined whisperings—
isolated chapters of William James written in mystic,
his mother the rival of time.

George Sandman

Our country could not nurse profit to health
nevermind the poems, novels—I have an old hairball.
I shall let everybody know. Goodbye now. Do not forget
Jean Cocteau. My book was
nothing more than a hole, some further impertinence.
Then it shrank into a mocking fairy
faking things normal people have—empty faces
to make people believe you are just like a person—
shape and making hobgoblins of the author.

The truth is that I am angry because I love everything
and spend my time dreaming of things never mentioned.

If I revenge myself in words
it is so I can almost feel
thought transmuting itself into existence
behind a mask in a kind of dream country of freak mythologies.

Well, the world is evil &
rich people don't understand nothing.
I gotta get back to work now.

A Cloud Atlas Is Hard to Find

Returning from my coffin, I saw myths facing backwards.
A gray monkey sprang into the Tennessee Waltz & said: "You can't win!"
I was the sorcerer just back from an eternal recurrence
trying to remember what it was I done.
I guess it was modernist love poetry to Starsky & Hutch with ironic
    deference to Wallace Stevens.
In the end it was no real pleasure.
I picked my nose, ordered myself the ghost of Christmas past in a
    cartoon Kung Fu pose
smiling up at the cloudless sky as if a snake took off his glasses.
Words grew ears filled with noises devoid of meaning
like sometimes a man says things he don't mean.
So I built a mound of stones for mem'ry—
the only one that ever raised the dead.

Journey to the End of Ulysses

It's hard to face an ape with a double chin
having just remembered the soft imps of ink in the squashed copybook.
Better than being ordinary, you thought
you had a fairy voice (of all the lousy luck),
a fluent croak toward mawkish forms of beauty—
a strange bumbling voice, absolutely indecent
you didn't dare speak
that fat gold refrain of shifted tomes, a lifted skirt at hip height,
the precise grace of a urinal (no harm in pleasure).

How's business? Murderers count the take with childish fingers.
Art? A beautiful book to be pissed on
(proceed to the nearest canteen).

Well, here's the penis & mathematics, nothing & another thing—
whistling a quandary as big as death.
"It's best to have it end like this," you said.
"My god I lost my breath yes that was why."

PROPHECIES FOR THE PAST

"… My parents
were a poetic
decision."
—Eileen Myles, "To the Maiden of Choices"

"What seems most outlandish in our
autobiography is what really happened."
—Steve Abbot, "Elegy"

On the day you're born your mother will think she's having a gall-bladder attack.

The night before, she'll put the finishing touches on a terrarium.

You'll imagine her sunburnt left arm placing a porcelain toadstool in the peat beneath a fern while a friend named Sid in a navy blue turtle-neck and white tennis shorts rattles the ice cubes in his gin and tonic after the uncomfortable silence that follows the obvious question, though that's not how it will happen, which will be beside the point. They're not your memories.

Your father, a homosexual, will wear a white polyester shirt with blue polka dots and a wide baby-blue paisley tie to their wedding in your mother's hospital bed. She'll have a blood clot. Their faces will state the obvious as they cut the cake: Surprise! Your father's face, you'll think, will betray the sad optimism of that personal moment in history that you'll later mistake for lies.

On the bed before them: a Navajo basket your mother will fill with buttons. You'll bury your hands in it, later, scrape the button edges across the memory of a cut on your thumb.

Sun-sparkled frost on a window pane grid; the chewed red satin edge of a Mickey Mouse blanket; the smell of lilac; a yellow wicker rocking chair; Scooby Doo in black and white; oatmeal in a Peter Rabbit bowl.

Your neighbors will raise rabbits for meat.

Carolyn, your mother's lover, will spank you. You won't remember. She'll apologize later in a letter, but you'll wish she hadn't.

You'll eat salted watermelon and squirrel; keep toads in a kiddy pool; hang catfish heads on chain link; collect cicada husks; drink milk with ice in Mason jars; hunt water moccasins with your grandmother on the farm where your father grew up in eastern Oklahoma.

You'll sing "The Greater is He That is in Me" at Panola Baptist Church in exchange for 13 silver dollars in a red velvet bag. The preacher will be named "Red." The carpet will be lime green. The baptismal font will be clear plexi-glass with a wallpaper scene of the Rocky Mountains behind it. You'll think it's called the "dismal font." You'll have a feeling that *The Bible* is bullshit, but not know why.

You'll watch your grandfather squash wasps with the pancake thumb he crushed as a rough neck; stare at the dentures he never wears that he keeps in a cup with his comb. The smell of Half & Half pipe tobacco, Beechnut spittle in Folger's spittoons at the cattle auction in Poteau.

You'll buy a beige Pac-Man t-shirt at a dime store in Solvang, wear it to the Hearst Castle.

You'll put your mother's dildo in a rollerskate, push it out into the living room where she'll be drinking tea with a psychologist named Bruce who'll later go by David.

You'll have a friend whose diet consists primarily of generic beef jerky, Lucky Charms and Tab Diet Cola. His mother, father, and stepmother will all have PhDs in Philosophy. Don't be jealous. He'll betray you.

Later, you'll go down on a girl in his hide-a-bed. She'll have her period, but you won't know it until you go out into the kitchen. There will be blood all over your face and your Wave Rave t-shirt. Everyone will laugh at you. You'll go to the refrigerator and take out a Tab.

You'll think about this when your father tries to tell you he has HIV.

You'll also wash your hands vigorously after his blood pools between your fingers when you swat a mosquito on the back of his leg.

You'll think you're the only one with a gay dad for years, but you aren't. Nevertheless, you'll feel a permanent loneliness you'll never fully articulate and never quite shake.

You'll hear a helicopter, a fly, mourning doves and a wind chime while you sit on the edge of the bed in your dead father's house, staring at a wicker rabbit when a finch hits the window.

For years you'll rinse the bathtub with a plastic cup with a pig on it from Central BBQ in Memphis, TN. You'll eat there with the parents of a friend from whom you'll buy a painting of amputees in underwear and wrestling masks skipping rope with a tar baby in a black buggy on a pink background.

You'll fall for an heiress from empires of both ready-to-bake, refrigerated pastries and instant cereals. She'll drink Diet Coke and smoke Marlboro lights, drive a navy blue Ford Escort station wagon, teach you how to flip a pencil around your thumb. You'll come as close as you'll ever get to understanding class, then snap under the pressure of your differences and leave her for the epileptic older sister of a childhood friend who has sex with you on a pale green chenille armchair covered in white dog hair while she talks on the phone to her mother. She'll teach you how to identify birds then leave you for a balding man who runs a nature camp. She'll leave him for another man you won't meet until years after she dies of a grand mal seizure while trying to get pregnant. He'll take you mushroom hunting.

The smells of lilac and Nerf football; Aim toothpaste, Margarita mix and wet Spring alley dirt in Dana Heffler's mouth.

Your first kiss will be with a girl who'll kill herself two years later with a cocktail of nail polish remover and asthma pills. You'll be 13 years old. You'll tuck a photo of yourself in your hockey uniform in her jacket pocket, touch her cold hand, see the stitches between her lips.

You'll light a birthday candle on the back of a Black Flag button, fall asleep and dream she comes halfway down the stairs of her house while you stand in the foyer. She'll say she's sorry and goodbye. Then she'll walk back upstairs into the black.

On the day your mother takes you to a nudist lesbian commune on a lake in the mountains, you'll slip off a picnic table and get a black eye so swollen you'll only be able to see the naked lesbians floating on inner-tubes through your left eye.

You'll notice your first pubic hair in the bathroom of an airplane, go back to your seat, order a ginger ale and think about a friend who borrowed a banana to prove that his boner was as big as a banana. You'll remember wondering what to do with that banana after he proved it.

You'll put it back in the bowl.

26 years later, you'll remember the same memory while admiring the lattice of frost crystals on the bird feeder in your backyard shortly after learning that your wife is pregnant with your second child. Then you'll remember the first time you ever jerked off: in the basement of your mother's friend's house while watching Joan Jett sing "I Love Rock & Roll" on MTV, which you'll also think about when you first read "Song of Myself."

You'll whisper "the body electric" under your breath while you look at your bookshelf and think about how, even though you can't remember much of what you read in all those books, you remember all the feelings and all the memories you had while reading them.

You'll remember reading *Jude the Obscure*, for example, after breaking up with the pastry/breakfast cereal heiress and feeling both prophetically understood and doomed all at once.

You'll like the idea that your body is a bookshelf full of people's best and most beautiful thoughts, but not their annoying personalities.

You'll make miniature dioramas in matchboxes and two sculptures: a dancing donut music box and an old spirit of turpentine bottle in which you'll place a little peach-colored plastic goon.

You'll hate yourself in ways you can live with, but can't entirely disown in art or poems, feel fake, shoulder a number of petty-but-cherished grudges through your days.

You'll have cheddar cheese, coffee and cigarettes near a satellite dish.

You'll play racquetball with a one-armed loan shark, build a 9-foot paper maché penis with friends and put it front of City Hall so you can watch the cops carry it away, talk knowingly about the "spankler plages" with Craig near a gigantic chair.

Later, you'll pack up everything you own, drive from Colorado Springs to New York, move into to a shitty third-floor walkup without a stove or toilet in Crown Heights above a half-way house for teenage trannies, commute 3 hours a day, watch your dog get run over, get bedbugs, get robbed, move back to Colorado Springs nine months later.

When you're eight, your best friend will pour orange juice over your head and call you "The Universe" over and over until you cry. You won't want to be the universe then; it will seem lonely and forbidding. Maybe later.

He'll have red shag clown carpet clotted with American cheese, yoghurt and toenails. You'll sneak his dad's *Penthouse* magazines in the front of your pants beneath your t-shirts and spread the centerfolds out while you listen to Dio.

Later, he'll drive his girlfriend's silver Rabbit through the front window of a Payless Shoe Source across the parking lot from a Wal-Mart.

In 6TH grade, you and Dane will try to get high by lighting a small pile of his brother's pot on the corner of his mother's pink sink with a match. You'll fan the smoke toward your face and huff like oracles of boredom, tongue his mother's Wild Turkey, spray Glade, eat crumpets and listen to the Scorpions' "Blackout" over and over on the record player.

In high school you'll get so stoned in the back of Scott's Mustang on the way to see the Scorpions at McNichols Arena that you won't be able to speak or move.

Years later, on your way back to college in Chicago, you'll get so high on hash that you'll realize you're driving down a sidewalk in Nebraska after buying a bowl of Chili at Wendy's.

You'll take acid, watch a brick wall turn into a teletype of hieroglyphs.

Later, you'll get so high and paranoid in the back seat of a drive-away hatchback Toyota Camry Mario will arrange to transport from San Francisco to New York that you'll be convinced you're on a cocaine smuggling run like in *Easy Rider*, except in a Toyota Camry.

He'll talk about the cold cuts in New Jersey all the way across the United States.

At the Illinois border, you'll get pulled over by a small-town cop in a shakedown for not having your windshield wipers on. Almost all the drugs you were transporting, it will turn out, will be yours. The cop will flush all your pills and keep your pot. Carl will joke with the cop while he gets fingerprinted. You'll take a picture while Phil, a little red balloon of dope still tucked beneath his tongue, does yoga on the floor. You'll get to Chicago before dark and stay with Steve, a con artist and the young lover of Don, an old professor, who'll come out at 59. Steve will have a big bag of blow like you imagined you were smuggling. Carl will do lines with him all evening while you try to shake the withdrawal in a paranoid bedroom haunted by a black velvet clown painting. You'll wake up around midnight refreshed; go to a corny SM dance club with Carl who'll pay to get his nipples waxed.

You'll get to New Jersey two days later, eat cold cuts, drive to Philly to see *Etant Donnés*.

You'll get to New York the next day, book a room at the Chelsea, do dexadrine with S. and A., envisage yourself, romantic and embarrassing, the poet in New York.

Two days later you'll interview Ron Padgett in his apartment on the lower East Side. He'll use the word "flood" metaphorically in regards to something about poetry just as a torrential downpour floods the hallway of his apartment building and water spills down the walls. You'll help him move his Joe Brainard pieces and bookcases away from the wall, then his wife will make you a balogna sandwich.

Many years later you'll pick him up from the airport in Colorado Springs for a reading. You'll take him to buy a bowl of potato soup at the Safeway where you learned to shoplift before you visit Kenward Elmslie's childhood home near Monument Valley Park. You'll talk about raccoons eating corn. After the reading, he'll order a scoop of vanilla ice cream and a decaf.

You and Mario will both have sex with your girlfriend one hot summer night in San Francisco not long after you get back from New York. It'll be the same day the man across the street who'll tell you that Janis Joplin lived in your apartment will die. You'll have been at a sex party in your old apartment on Valencia where everyone will stand around the blue bathtub to watch your former roommates' girlfriend get worked over with a gigantic black dildo. It'll seem strangely ordinary, almost boring. You'll cheat on your girlfriend with a poet in the dirt behind a log above the old Sutro Baths at Ocean Beach. You'll still love her, but she won't believe you enough not to leave. And you won't love her enough to stop her. She'll move to Barcelona. You'll fly out to try and patch things up, eat blood sausage and Frosted Flakes for breakfast, smoke hash in the streets as you marvel at the strange, small cars, nevermind Gaudí. You'll never see her again.

Mario will study Kung Fu, become a Muslim, have an arranged marriage in Morocco, bug your gay Mexican Jewish poet friend about going straight to save his soul. You'll never see him again.

You'll be the fourth man hired to work at a women-owned sex toy store in the Mission. You'll juggle dildos on the zebra-striped carpet near the phone banks, review porn and sex toys, meet wonderfully peculiar queers.

You'll drive the U-Haul moving van for a staged consensual abduction and rape on Polk Street arranged by a friend who'll like to play Boy Scouts. She won't cut off her tits or take testosterone because she'll know something about neitherness. You'll never speak of it. You'll identify with her more than anyone else you'll ever know, but remain the watcher. You'll help her write a chapbook about a can of pork.

Years later you'll see two dykes hotboxing Virginia Slims in the cab of a Dodge Dakota with a camper top and think about her at a stoplight near the Atmel semi-conductor fabrication corporation where Craig will work. He'll tell you stories about people fucking in the corridors outside the clean rooms on the night shift. Later that same day you'll see a transvestite cowboy whose face was badly disfigured as a child. He'll be buying lumber at Home Depot. You'll recognize him from a tranny support meeting you'll go to while working on an article about a transsexual who'll lose custody of her children after she transitions. She'll live in trailer park with a parrot.

Later, you'll interview Stanley Biber—the sex change doctor of Trinidad, Colorado. It'll be his last interview. Small, bald and macho, he'll tell you he did it because he could. But this is later.

Earlier, in college, you'll smoke cigarettes with the pigeons in the *plakas* of Athens, walk the olive groves on Crete, lie on your back beneath the dome of Hagia Sophia. You'll get flashed by a wanker in a park outside Ephesus, propositioned by a leather vendor who'll offer you a huge joint in Izmir, wonder at the many breasts of Artemis. You'll listen to the sands crackle while you float on your back in the Aegean at Monemvasia, your dad not yet dead.

Also: a professor, mostly mustache, will fuck a student and get her pregnant. Another gets ALS, lets his wife fuck someone else and watches.

You'll see Gun 'N' Roses twice in college: Once on acid with Dane and Avery. Afterwards, Avery won't be able to stop talking about how it wouldn't matter if he "just killed someone." He'll have just read Camus. You'll remind him that he also just saw Poison and Guns 'N' Roses while you sit in a booth across from some cops at a Denny's. Dane will barf on your truck. You'll make him wash it off with the hose while you wear his dad's coyote pelt; the second time in Athens at Olympic Stadium. You won't have tickets, but John will say he knows the band and they'll believe him, which he'll credit to the many years he spent taking acid.

After college, you'll move to Bogotá to look after an 8-year old with cerebral palsy. Four men will get gunned down in a black BMW outside the school where you'll study Spanish just minutes after you leave. Dumb luck will follow you. You'll cross the *páramo* from San Augustín to Popayán on top of a jeep with Kit whose sun-blistered face will get caked in red dust.

Later, you'll end up living on the floor of an ashram with a swami who'll think lesbians eat too many eggs. You'll drink your own piss, pose nude for an angry middle–aged sculptor who'll invite you to a hut on a banana plantation near a lagoon full of crocodiles outside Tyrona, then to Cartegena under the pretense of poaching coral for her awful sculptures. She'll want you to get her pregnant. You'll pretend you're too into Yoga when she throws herself at you in an open silk kimono. She'll scream at you and gnash her teeth when you redouble your refusals. You'll spend the next day pretending to meditate on a small island full of washed-up flip-flops.

Later, you'll get really high and dance with Joanne Kyger on New Year's Eve in Morelia while traveling with Daniel and Danielle. At Zipolite you'll whine about your sleeping bag, get bored at the beach, spend the night with a couple of locals in an Acapulco strip club.

You'll read *Moby Dick* on the Zephyr from San Fransisco to Denver with Mike and Ed. In the lounge car, you'll meet a truck driver with terminal cancer. He'll buy you drinks all the way to Reno where, he'll tell you, he plans to spend the rest of his days in a whore house. Ed'll get sick on Christmas. Your mom will give him a purple hat.

In high school, you'll drive to the Mall of the Bluffs to watch Stevie Velasquez fight a linebacker from the Doherty High School football team. He'll tack the cuffs of his acid-washed jeans above his Zodiac loafers and run a Goody brush through his black mullet, spin it around his finger, tuck it in his back pocket. He'll duck the first punch and end the fight with a single kick to the side of the head. There will be blood in the linebacker's ear. Stevie will tack his cuffs and brush his hair again. "Beating people up can be beautiful," you'll think, remembering the fight 20 years later.

In Jr. High you'll get your ass kicked by a kid named Tommy who you'll call a retard. He'll show up in a brand new Motley Crüe t-shirt, punch you in the forehead on the bike path after school before Shane breaks it up with karate. You'll deserve it. It will be one among the myriad regrets against which you'll strain to defend yourself with the soft clay fists of insomnia … forsaken helmets, untended frienships and embarrassing masks you'll mistake for your face.

You won't know it at the time, but you'll often see a strange looking girl in a cheerleader's outfit on that bike path who many will later accuse of being a deluded con man posing as Kathy Ireland's niece. You'll recognize something in her longing as she stares at the North Jr. High School Viking cheerleaders, but won't know why. She'll get caught "impersonating a student." at your high school the year after you graduate. Her birth name will be Charles Daugherty. Then, for years, you'll follow her story with great interest as she dupes dozens of people into believing that she's a super model. You'll hope to interview her, believing her to be an unacknowledged folk hero and secret sharer of your hidden life. At her last competency hearing you'll learn that she was born a hermaphrodite and given a boy's name even though she never had sexual reassignment surgery and later wanted to be a girl. They'll send her to the Colorado State Mental Hospital in Pueblo. No one but you, you'll think, will seem to understand why she had such a spectacular fantasy life. You'll never get an interview.

When you're 21, shortly before your father dies, he'll tell you that he first had sex with an older man in the bathroom of the public library in Wilburton, Oklahoma, when he was 8 years old and that he liked it as you both watch muddy flood waters spill through the arroyos in Sabino Canyon.

Later, you'll understand the personal and political histories he was up against, but you'll never fully forgive him. You'll give yourself to your son in every way your father never did, hoping to salvage some measure of redemption from the pain. It won't occur to you that it's your father you're trying to redeem.

You'll often think about his last hours, your mind thrashing in the web of tubes in which you'll watch him wither to bone. "The stars like billygoats," you'll write later, trying to browbeat the answer out of his new absence, just as likely stupid, full of feelings in dead language …

At the moment he dies, a skeletal finger will reach out through the black in your dreams to turn off a blank TV. David will knock on the window to tell you he's dead.

You'll feel so terribly lost looking back at the empty outlines of these memories, the years through which anger will drag you as you rake through the vanishing details:

They'll serve lobster bisque after the funeral.

The orange Post-It Notes your grandmother and aunt will paste on everything in the house they think they deserve. Your grandmother will blame your dad's partner for everything. He'll tear all the Post-Its off after they leave.

Two years later, after returning from Colombia, you'll get dengue fever, almost die, go live with your dad's partner in their house on Drennan. He'll have cancer and a new lover almost 20 years younger. You'll listen to them fuck sometimes, work at a Mormon health food store, meet a poet who'll confess to killing her lover.

At 24 you'll move to San Francisco, meet a charming junkie beneath a magnolia tree in North Berkeley, heave your last sigh of idealism for poetry.

You'll photocopy magazines at the dump, print a precious all-night book about donuts.

You'll sleep in a closet in which Carl will paint a giant vagina, drink Miller Lite beneath a palm tree in Kevin's back yard in Palo Alto.

You'll buy a pound of weed. It'll get moldy.

In L.A. on speed: Katie won't take dictation, but she'll want to fuck you. Rick will be OK with it, but it never happens.

You'll meet Marina through Darin at a book show in the Mission, get pregnant at a hippy hot springs in Calistoga, move in together on Natoma Street with a cobbler who'll make shoes for drag queens. You'll be poor, but happy.

You'll move back to Colorado Springs, live in a little purple cottage on a weedy hill near the Jr. High School where Erin will have kicked you in the balls.

Memories will crowd the streets:

Eating plums in a tree on Nevada Avenue all afternoon with a Jehovah's Witness named Jordan. He'll wear a navy blue turtleneck and white tennis shorts. You'll want to ask him what it's like to not get presents, but neither of you will say anything.

Learning to smoke from a neighborhood kid whose mom's a dyke, too. You won't inhale and he'll call you a pussy behind the woodpile then puke an ashen bile before it's time to leave for Chuck E. Cheese's.

Hot dogs with Mac 'n' Cheese in parquet wooden bowls at Josh's house on Boulder Street; bad acne on 31ST where you'll have sex for the first time in the basement at the end of a Broncos game; the Safeway on Wahsatch where you'll get caught shoplifting a Vick's nasal inhaler.

You'll want moon boots, a lawn.

Cille Burns' apartment on Columbia Street where you'll spend Sundays listening to Earth, Wind & Fire records, eating collard greens and pork ribs. You'll sink down into the brown paisley couch that wafts chitlins and pot smoke, tiptoe to the cable box to watch The Playboy Channel. You'll listen for the waterbed slosh, Cille's filthy bunny slipper shuffle, roach clip in the tin on the fridge next to the whiskey. You won't know they're lovers until later. "Black is Beautiful."

Your mom will tell you that it isn't really like that—like it is on the Playboy Channel, but you won't want to talk about it because you'd prefer that it would be like that. An activist for abortion rights and feminist health care, she'll bring home multi-colored lubricated condoms for birthday balloons. They'll get covered in cat hair. She'll defend you from the separatists and your father's promises, never live with lovers just in case. The hiding and passing will be understood as necessity.

More than anything you'll remember 11. Your mom will take you to San Francisco on vacation where you'll see: a Japanese couple eat dinner naked at a glass banquet table; men with moustaches French kissing; a young Aphrodite's dazzling diamond breasts in the surf off Angel

Island; a Castro clone with pierced nipples and a tub of Vaseline jacking off on a brown shag carpet beneath a strobe through the skylight from Myra's balcony near Bernal Hill. Mom will tell you Myra's trying to get pregnant and explain it in such a way that all you'll remember is a Seven Dwarves Dixie cup and a turkey baster.

"Do you know anyone else who's a lesbian," she'll ask you when the trip is over. You'll be in the San Francisco airport listening to "Bitchin' Camaro" on your Walkman when she taps you on the shoulder. You'll think she's being trendy when she says it—think the word "lesbian" sounds stupid. She'll tell you dad's queer, too. You'll know it's true, remember the *Joy of Gay Sex* you'll find beneath his bed a few months earlier and how you tried not to think about it while you stared at the grapefruits floating in the swimming pool.

You're the dumbest detective, you'll think, hate your brand-new blue-and-white checkerboard Vans.

Six years later, you'll be at the coffee shop in the Tucson airport where you'll stare at the plastic-wrapped row of Hustlers on the magazine rack while your father tries to tell you he has HIV.

The tabletops will be orange Formica.

You'll already know because your mother will have told you a year earlier.

You'll just want him to say it.

But he won't say it.

Why won't he just say it?

You'll wish he would just say it.

That's when you'll think about the blood all over your face, and that Tab Diet Cola, and all the years of silence and forgetting. You'll wish you could make sense of any of it, rearrange the memories.

But you won't have time for anything more than these shapeless thumbnails.

Stick it in the time machine and set the date:

September 2, 1972.

Acknowledgments

Many thanks to Julien Poirier and Ugly Duckling Presse for asking and for taking this on; to Kevin Opstedal for publishing my poems all these years so beautifully; to Marina Eckler, Craig Richardson and Alysia Abbott for the invaluable feedback; to Mom and Pam for everything; and to Matt Barton for the Tough Shed residency.

When I first saw Noel Black, he was sitting at his messy desk in the newspaper's offices. If I hadn't known it was impossible, I would have thought that there were blades of grass sprouting on his face. As I'd entered, a young homosexual man had been leaving. Noel afforded, "My dad was gay. And so was my mom." "So, it's hereditary?" I asked. "Fuck no, you ignorant shit," he replied, "I'm gay because of this stuff on my face." "You mean it makes you more shy with girls than with men?" "What are you, an idiot? No—it's sperm, and I like having it there!"

—Richard Hell

Noel Black lives with his wife and two sons in Colorado Springs.